101 Secret Hiding Places

How to Secure Your Treasures

by Tristan Trubble

Published in USA by:

Tristan Trubble
P.O BOX #9
Boynton Beach
FL 33425

© Copyright 2016

ISBN-13: 978-1539994565
ISBN-10: 1539994562

Table of Contents

Chapter 2: Travel Security : Hiding Valuables Away From Home

Introduction

Sometimes the secret to stashing your valuables is as simple as a hollowed out book. In other cases, whatever it is you're intending to protect may be highly confidential information that requires increased security. A hollow book just won't do. This book isn't hollow; in it, we will discuss various hiding places, from the simple and straight forward to the complex – a place to hide your cash from your light-fingered roommate or a place where your family heirlooms may be safe from the most cunning of jewelry thieves. We will also look at secret hiding places specific to travel, as tourists are often a prime target for petty theft or burglary.

The use of secret hiding places isn't limited to hiding items of value; hiding places can also be used to conceal weapons. Carrying a weapon on your person at all times will allow you to defend yourself should the need arise, without provoking suspicion in your assailant or making those around you feel threatened. We'll provide a few methods by which to hide both valuables and weapons on your person.

Technology has brought with it a transparency that's both good and bad, depending on how you look at it. It's good in that society has every bit of information at their fingertips; it's bad in that everyone knows your business – especially if you have an online presence. Keeping things hidden doesn't have to end at physical property; it can include hiding your personal information or online footprint as well. For this reason, we've incorporated methods by which to hide yourself and your tracks on the Internet.

As a whole, this book will discuss how to hide things that you value from those who wish to rob you of them. To hide something from a thief, you'll need to think like a thief. Understanding their motivations will allow you to deduce what they might target first. Your average house thief or identity thief will have two basic motivations: to steal anything of value and to escape before being caught. One important thing to remember when creating any secret hiding place is that whoever is so absolutely determined to uncover your valuables will search and search until they've landed on something of worth. To prevent them from overturning your life, you might create a false stash to throw them off, which will get your thief to quit while he's ahead (or thinks that he is, anyway).

If a thief cannot find money or something of value to steal in the places that one might expect to find them, your house will likely be torn to pieces in the search for something to make his breaking-and-entering worth the potential consequences (ie, arrest and jail time). So when it comes to securing your secret hiding places throughout your home, offering up a "fake" teaser stash in a more obvious place may ensure further protection, as your thief might take your offering and leave. For instance, if you're hiding documents or photos, place some fake ones "on file" in your home filing cabinet, so that your thief gets away with nothing but stock photos and fraudulent information. If you're stashing a significant amount of money and valuables in your home, place a hundred bucks in your bedside cabinet or some 14 karot gold jewelry in a lockbox. Make your thieves believe they got off with your valuables when really they didn't even scratch the surface. You might also consider keeping a file titled "Bank Safe Deposit Box" on hand with a fake list of valuables that are "stored" elsewhere. Thus, if your thief isn't one of your run-of-the-mill dummies, he will deduce from the evidence that you "provided" that your money is stored elsewhere.

Safes, though not so much "secret" as quite obvious hiding places, are a good investment for those who are looking to store valuables for the long-term. They provide quality security with the added benefit of being damn near impossible to move. Unless you are the target of some kind of sting, your average thief is not going to spend time trying to bust a safe open, being that one of their primary aims is to get the job done as quickly as possible.

In the end, however, you can design your own quality security simply by coming up with creative secret hiding places that would take a thief, crafty and cunning as a fox, to uncover.

4

Chapter 1:
Secret "Safes": Hiding
Valuables in Your Home

#1 Junction Box

You can use an empty, unused junction box to produce a nice sized hiding place to stash your goods. Because it's a permanent fixture that one might normally see in a home, your thief won't think anything of it, and especially wouldn't consider that you've hidden something within. To make your fake junction box look like the real deal, you'll need drywall screws, a screw gun, scrap rollnex wire, plastic cable connectors, and wire snips or sheers. Salvage a used junction box from the dump and, with your screw gun and drywall screws, screw it to a piece of ply wood up near the floor joints, where a real junction box would normally be placed. Then snip off three or four different lengths of wires to insert into the junction box. Add bushings hardware connects, to the junction box and thread your fake (non-live) wire through the box. Drill a couple of holes into the wood near the junction box and feed the other ends of the wires into the holes, caulking them in place, to make it look as though they're running electricity somewhere. Place your valuables inside the box, screw the cover in place, and there you have it – a secret safe hiding in plain sight.

#2 Thermostat

Similarly to the junction box, you can create a small hideaway fake-out with an old thermostat. Though it'll provide less room to store things, you might hide small pieces of jewelry, cash, or documents via a USB within the mini-safe. Simply hollow out the inside, fill it with whatever it is you want to stash, and secure it to a wall in your home.

#3 Electrical Outlet

A fake electrical outlet is another permanent fixture that will provide you a convenient hiding place that'd be damn near impossible for a thief to find. Install a non-wired electrical outlet or a cable outlet wherever it won't be an eyesore and hide your small treasures within. A cable outlet works best, because the coax plug will work double-time as a handle to open your outlet, while the innards of the coax cable outlet provide more room to store stuff than an electrical outlet.

#4 PVC Drain

A basement with a bunch of PVC piping can provide you a labyrinth in which to store your valuables, including important documents. Search for a spot to install your fake PVC drainpipe near a utility sink, perhaps beside a real drainpipe. Using a hacksaw, cut a 3 inch PVC pipe however long you wish (maybe not too long; about 12 inches). This will give you plenty of room to store some valuables without the pipe potentially tipping over from the weight. Cut a 2 inch PVC pipe into one 2 inch piece and one 4 inch piece, and cut a 1 inch PVC pipe into a 6 inch piece. Using a 4 inch to 3 inch PVC Sewer Drain Adaptor, assemble the fake drainpipe. Fit the 4 inch to 3 inch adaptor to the 12 inch PVC pipe, and fit the 4 inch piece of PVC pipe between the Wye (Y) adaptor and the 3 inch to 2 inch adaptor. Put an end cap on the 1 inch pipe and fit it onto the Wye (Y) adaptor. The 2 inch piece of PVC will connect the PVC clean out plug and the top of the Wye (Y) adaptor. Glue the pieces together and caulk the drainpipe base adaptor to the floor. Put all of the valuables you wish to stow into an airtight bag and fit it into the 12 inches of 3 inch PVC pipe for safe keeping.

#5 Doortop Stash

[photo credit: <u>diyncrafts</u>]

An easy project that'll take no more than a few minutes and yet would take ages for a cunning thief to discover is this hidden doortop stash. The interior of inside doors is often hollow, so you can easily drill a hole the same diameter as your container – a cigar box or tube, for instance – and place the container within your doortop. Positioning the container flush with the top of your door, you can lift the container out by using a strong magnet. Common thieves will not think to search a door's interior, so you can hide either a small stash or a decent amount of valuables within your door.

#6 Fake Phone Jack

Yet another everyday permanent fixture, a fake phone jack will allow you to store USB data within your wall. Simply create a USB cord with a phone jack terminal connected to one end and wire it to a phone plate. This will allow you access to your secret files where no thief will be likely to find them.

#7 Freezed Foil

You can foil your burglar by wrapping money or valuables in aluminum foil and burying them in the freezer. Though your burglar may have the discourtesy to tear through your house, it's unlikely that he'll be so rude as to pick through your "food," making your fridge or freezer one of the safest places to stash your stuff.

#8 Painted Mayonnaise Jar

Another way to store valuables amongst your foods is to fill your fridge or pantry with mason jars. Just as thieves are unlikely to open your freezer and pick through aluminum foil, they are just as unlikely to open your mason jars if the contents on the inside appear in line with the label. A great advantage to this secret hiding place is that a large mason jar can hide a considerable amount of valuables. You might consider going with an old mayonnaise jar, as the color of mayonnaise will be easy to match with paint. Wash it out and coat the inside evenly with off-white paint, ensuring that the paint is thick enough to appear real. Leave the lid off the jar and let it dry, then fill it with whatever valuables you wish to conceal.

#9 False Electrical Panel

A false electrical panel is another fantastic storage option for larger valuables. Again, being a permanent fixture in many homes, the panel will be invisible to the naked eye...or at least to the eye of a thief, who won't see it as anything but a panel. Invest in an electrical panel and install it in your basement or garage. Place a sticker that reads "high voltage" on the door, and keep the panel under lock and key so that even members of your household cannot access it (if you should so choose to keep this hiding place a secret even from them). Not many thieves will go near your electrical panel, not simply because it appears inconspicuous, but because the seeming danger of electric shock would put them off.

#10 Curtain Pocket

Your curtains aren't only practical for hiding from the sun, they're practical when it comes to hiding your possessions as well. Documents, cash, and other flat items can be stitched into your curtains seamlessly, without an undiscerning eye knowing any differently. Simply select a curtain (or a material out of which to make your own set of curtains) that won't betray a hidden compartment and sew a pocket into the backside of the curtain, using thread whose stitches cannot be seen on the opposite side. If you've selected an already manufactured curtain, you'll have to find material that matches, whereas if you've made your own, you already have the material on hand. Store emergency funds or anything flat that's of value within the pocket.

#11 False Ductwork

Large items can be hidden through using false ductwork as a concealer. Simply run some extra HVAC in your basement or crawl space – wherever there's ductwork already constructed – and hide your belongings within. Just remember which is false and which is the real thing.

#12 Soil of a Plant

Plants can do more than give some semblance of nature inside your home; the potted plant may turn out to be a life-saver when it comes to storing your valuables. The fake soil of a fake plant is a great place to bury your valuables for safe-keeping, as your burglar will not likely give foliage a second glance. Simply place your valuables in a ziploc bag or container, bury it in the potted plant, and cover with soil.

#13 Picture Frame

Though thieves may search behind the picture frame, they don't often take the time to open the back, making this a safe place to store paper-thin valuables. You might store cash or documents between a photo and the cardboard backing of the picture frame. Rest assured that your thief will be none too bright to check more than the backside of your frame.

#14 Inside a Toy

A kid's room is often the last place a burglar will search for anything of value, so this is the perfect place to store valuables for the short-term. Find a toy that has an inner compartment and hide your valuables inside of it. Not only do burglars rarely ever enter a child's room, but it's highly improbable that one would pick out your toy from the thousands that litter the floor.

#15 Inside a Bottle of Aspirin or Other Container

If you have a wad of cash that you want to hide away, you might consider storing it inside an aspirin bottle or other small container, like a can of soup or a box of tea. Though your house guest with a headache may come upon your stash naturally, a burglar will not race directly to your medicine cabinet for headache medicine and won't conclude that you must have stored your valuables in there.

#16 In a Book

If you have a library of books, this option works especially well. You can place money or documents inside of your favorite hardback and leave your intruders to search through every single leaf out of hundreds of books. Unless they're a literature buff and decide to take a gander at Moby Dick while they're on the job, it's highly unlikely that they'll come across your hidden treasure. However, don't place valuables in DVD cases or the like, as thieves will often make off with these, whether they've found your secret stash within the case or not.

#17 Hollowed Out Book

Otherwise known as a booksafe, a hollowed out book is easy to make and can hold thicker valuables than the above-mentioned book option is capable of holding. In fact, rather than buy a ready-made booksafe, you can make your own. Simply find a large book that holds no sentimental value and, opening your chosen book about 50 pages in, use a box cutter to slice a compartment into the pages. Create about an inch of a border on the outer edges, and cut deep enough to hold your valuables.

#18 False Bottoms

Though hiding valuables in your rolled up socks may be a thing of the past – one too obvious to be a secret any longer – you can still make use of your sock drawer, or any drawer, as a source of concealment. All you have to do is take an empty drawer, find a thin piece of wood with the same wood grain or another similar-looking but sturdy material, measure and cut that piece to the same dimensions as your drawer bottom, place flat documents or valuables in the bottom of the drawer, and cover them with the false bottom. Who would guess there's anything but socks in your drawer? Neither a thief nor your housekeeper will know the difference.

#19 Under Floorboards

Though this method is rather common, prying up the floorboards in search of valuables is not something just any old thief would do, unless he has reason to believe you've stored valuables beneath the floor. Just be sure to avoid placing precious metals, firearms, ammunition, or coins in this secret hiding place, as a clean sweep with a metal detector will reveal your stash in seconds.

#20 In Walls

Just as with floorboards, if you have a way to create a hidden compartment in the hollow of a wall without hindering the integrity of your home's structure, then do it to it. Creating this hiding place may involve including a false back to a shelf, behind which you can hide your valuables in the wall, or creating a hidden door flush to the wall, camouflaged behind wall paper. Or, if you're storing valuables for the long-term, you can go so far as to drywall them in. Whatever your imagination can think up, with a few tools, materials, and a little ingenuity, you can probably produce it.

#21 Under Aquarium Rocks

Home invaders may be careless enough to smash things, but they don't often wish to get their hands dirty...or at least, they wouldn't expect *you* to do so when hiding valuables, making any place messy or wet a great secret hiding place. And so enters the aquarium into the mix. Whether it be an aquarium that houses fishes, snakes or a gigantic Tarantula, you can place your valuables inside a waterproof container or plastic bag and hide them beneath the rocks of your pet's flooring, a place truly difficult to access and not so clean either.

#22 Attic Insulation

Your home may have a full walk-in attic or it may simply have a cramped space, filled with fiberglass, spiders, mice, dust and other nasty material. Believe it or not, the latter may be safer to store your valuables in as, again, your common thief isn't looking to get his hands dirty or leave tracks. If you choose to hide your goods amongst the insulation, be sure to contain them securely in an airtight bag and, when placing them, don't leave your own tracks in the dust.

#23 Mouldings

Windows, countertops, cabinetry at floor level, and many other built-in arrangements have wall guards or moulding. You can modify these with strong magnets or hinges to create secret hiding places behind access panels.

#24 Stair Steps

A quite large and easily accessible storage space, stair steps look unobtrusive but are well built for hiding stuff in, as access panels can be easily introduced into your steps and are virtually invisible to the naked eye. When creating this secret hiding place, however, ensure that the stair doesn't sound hollow when trod upon, as this may give a burglar reason to believe there's something inside. Also, secure the fake step so that it won't get kicked in or trip people up when stampeding up and down the stairs.

#25 Hollowed Out Table Leg

An oldie, yet a goody, hollowed out items have served their purpose for centuries as places to hide the secretest of secrets. And when you think about it, this hiding place makes perfect sense; after all, who would think twice about your average table leg or bedpost. Not even the savviest of thieves would jump to the conclusion that it is, in fact, hollowed out when, in all actuality, it could conceal everything from wads of cash to rolled up documents to your family jewels. The heavy lifting involved in examining a table (especially a pool table) would likely dissuade thieves from doing anything more than looking under it to see if valuables have been stored beneath the tabletop.

#26 Hollow Clock

Whether you purchase a hollow wall clock specifically designed to store your valuables or you create your own, this hidden compartment is a convenient place to store hanging jewelry or other important items. Just make sure the clock works so that your more clever of thieves don't get suspicious that time is not running out.

#27 In an Air Vent

By installing a fake air vent, you can easily hide things in a hidden compartment behind your wall. All you need to do is cut out a section of drywall, place a compartment inside, set a black divider against the grill frame, so that no one can spot your stuff, even if they look closely, and fasten the air vent onto the wall with screws. It's as simple as that. Now you have a good sized secret hiding place to store everything from piles of confidential documents to family heirlooms.

#28 In the Toe Kicks of Cabinets

Kitchen cabinets are often fitted with toe kicks – 4 inch tall cavities beneath the cabinets. Instead of allowing this area to be dead space, use an oscillating tool to pull off the plywood of the toe kicks, which is often only ¼ of an inch thick, to make them removable. Then fit the toe kick with round hook-and-loop self adhesive tape. Place your valuables in the free space and press the toe kicks back in place.

#29 Bed Safe

[photo credit: safewise]

Long gone are the days where hiding valuables under the mattress was the norm...or maybe not. With a bed safe, you'll still be hiding stuff under a mattress, but the box bed will look like a bed frame. This secret safe under your mattress brings a whole new meaning to hiding things under the bed. The safe has plenty of room for all of your valuables, big and small, and is secured even further with locks.

#30 Bedpost

Similar to the hollowed out table leg, a hollowed out bedpost serves its purpose well by hiding your valuables in plain sight. Whether you're working with a thick wooden bedpost or iron bars, both can be easily manipulated to hide your belongings within. Iron bars may already be hollow inside, while you can hollow out wooden posts with a drill bit and fit the top or bottom of the hole with a camouflaged cover up piece of wood.

#31 False Flammables

Hiding valuables in a fake "flammable" container – like a gasoline can or anything that screams "Warning!" – is a good way to keep thieves on their toes. Not only will the container seem completely inconspicuous, but thieves will probably want to steer clear of anything that has the potential to light things up.

#32 In a Vacuum Cleaner

Being that intruders who are looking to steal your stuff aren't likely to turn over a new leaf in the process of their burglary and do some housework for you, vacuum cleaners – or other household cleaners – are a safe bet for safe storage. If you have an old disused vacuum cleaner, remove the bag and replace it with your own ziplocked bag of valuables. This way, you'll have easy access to your storage, while burglars will be none the wiser.

#33 Between Upper Cabinets

The upper cabinets in a kitchen often have a ½ inch gap between each pair, perfect to slip a manila envelope of money or important documents from view. You can secure the envelope to the sides of the cabinet tops with binder clips so that your important information doesn't slip between the cracks. Unless your thief comes through the air vent in the ceiling, they're unlikely to spot the hidden treasure.

#34 In Appliance Grills

Kitchen appliances, like dishwashers or refrigerators, are fitted with a snap-off grill in the front, and the space inside has coils but is often fairly cavernous, providing plenty of room to hide your goods. Put your goods in an airtight container and stash them behind the appliance grill, making sure that your container is not blocking the airflow, which might damage your appliance.

#35 Paint Can Storage

What kind of thief is going to pry open your standard paint can in beige expecting to find gold? Not many will think to look amongst the junk piled in a corner of your garage which reeks of paint and, thus, could easily track their fingerprints. Empty a paint can and fill it with your valuables then super glue it shut, so that it's even more inaccessible to those nasty villains.

#36 In Upholstery

Unless your burglar feels there's reason to literally tear open your furniture, they won't ever find the valuables sewn inside. If you're a handy seamstress, you can easily cut into the fabric back of a couch, fit some cash or other valuables within, and sew it back up so that it looks as good as new. Or simply unzip your chair or couch cushion and hide your things within the foam padding, perhaps designing your own padding by sandwiching your goods between two pieces and sewing or otherwise sealing these pieces together.

#37 False Lampshade

If you have important documents to store, you can do so within the lining of a lampshade. Simply seal two lampshade cones together (the inner one a bit smaller than the outer) with your documents fixed in between. If you need to hide a hard copy of your granny's will from your cutthroat relatives, this may be the way to go.

#38 Under the House

There are two options to storing goods under the house: either between floor joists or buried in the dirt. If your thieves are trying to do a quick, clean job of it, they aren't going to want to crawl under your house and wade through the dark and the damp. In fact, damp spots are especially good options for storage, as they are extremely unpleasant to search. Keep your stuff in waterproof containers so that it isn't affected by the conditions. You can add pipes or insulation between the joists to further camouflage the goods. You can also bury your treasure beneath your house near floor supports or foundations, if the crawl space has a dirt floor. Again, ensure that your valuables are sealed in an airtight waterproof container.

#39 In the Garden

Buried treasure ain't just for pirates. Your garden is another option if you choose to dig in the dirt to hide your goods. Put your valuables in a medicine bottle or waterproof container and bury them where you can find them, perhaps beneath a specific stone or garden bench.

This option is not a good idea if you have an animal that likes to dig. In that case, your treasure won't stay buried for long.

#40 Lockable Trap Door in Linen Closet

In the unlikely event that your intruder decides to go rummaging through your linen closet, they're going to grow frustrated pretty quickly when piles and piles of towels and linen turn up nothing. They'll be so frustrated that they won't see the trap door that you've so cleverly hidden behind the shelves. This hiding place will work especially for those who are planning on doing some remodeling. Leaving space for hidden storage at the back of any closet will allow you to get creative with your renovation and produce a storage space that's large and well hidden from view

Chapter 2:
Travel Security : Hiding
Valuables Away From Home

On the Plane

#41 Fake Toiletries

You're only allowed two ounce bottles in your toiletry bag, but these two ounces are significant enough for pieces of jewelry or a roll of dough that you don't want stolen at the airport. As your purse will most often be a thief's first target, your toiletry bag is a safe haven in which to store your valuables.

#42 Interior Lining of Suitcase

Though the zippered pockets of your suitcase are easy enough to access, homemade pockets sewn or otherwise fitted into the lining of your suitcase won't be easily distinguishable even to the most astute of thieves. Create a hidden sleeve in the sides of your bag, lined with velcro, so that you can lift the fabric off and get at the cash, cards or important documents stored within.

#43 Travel Notebook

Travel notebooks often have a pocket within which you may store little scraps of mementos from your trip. Instead of using this pocket for mementos, utilize this space to store that little extra emergency cash to be used in the event that your other funds are stolen. Unless your thief is interested in that pretty sunset you watched over the Mediterranean or your trek along the Great Wall, a travel notebook is not likely his go-to steal.

On Public Transport

#44 Travel Pouch

A travel pouch is attached to a long thread so that you might hang it around your neck or on your shoulder underneath your clothing. Often fitted with zippered pockets to store cash, credit cards, tickets and your passport, a travel pouch is a nifty alternative to a purse when you're on stuffy, overcrowded public transport. Most will assume it's only a necklace. Just be sure to wear it beneath your clothing where no one can see it.

#45 Scarf

A classy scarf can do double-duty, serving your style and security. You can either use a scarf lined with secret pockets to store your valuables in or use it as a safe-tie for your purse or camera. If a thief tries to do a snatch and run, he won't get far if you've secretly tied your scarf to your valuables. The fact that your scarf is tied around your neck and often tucked into your coat or jacket means that your valuables are in one of the safest of places on your person.

#46 Inner Pockets

When you're on public transport, any pocket on the outside of your garment is, quite literally, up for grabs. But when it's inside your coat or jacket, then it's simply impossible to get too, especially if you're zipped up from waist to chin. These secret compartments are often already designed into many outer wear garments, but if yours is without them, inner pockets are easy enough to make yourself, being that the hiding place often involves a simple sewing of a square pocket of fabric into the interior lining of your garment.

In Your Hotel Room

#47 Under the Bottom Dresser Drawer

If you remove the bottom dresser drawer of your

hotel room's nightstand, you'll often find that there's a decent amount of space in which to store valuables. Utilize this space to hide everything from your emergency funds to your valuable jewelry. It may even be large enough to slide your iPad or computer into.

#48 Envelope in Obscure Places

Take an envelope and tape along with you to your hotel – it'll come in handy when you want to stash money or documents in your room. You can tape your goods to the bottom of drawers, inside bi-fold doors, under chairs, behind appliances that are up against a wall, or in any other area of the room that is obscure and not regularly cleaned.

#49 In the Shower Rod

If you pop one side of the shower rod off of its holding, you can stash valuables within the hollow of the rod. Simply wrap your valuables in a plastic bag, slide them into the rod, and put the rod back in place. Even if your housekeepers are honest saints, they won't possibly discover or disturb your curtain rod safe.

In High Traffic Areas

#50 Money Belt

When it comes down to it, the money belt was built specifically for travel security, so even if you feel a bit foolish wearing it, the money belt is indeed a foolproof secret hiding place when it comes to walking around high traffic areas, where those light-fingered pickpockets often linger. Attached around the waist and hidden beneath your shirt or pants, the belt is not easily accessible by pickpockets and will go unnoticed by prying eyes, searching for anything of value that you carry. Often with two separate pockets, you can hide your money, credit cards, and passport on you at all times, as close as humanly possible to your being.

Chapter 3:
Concealed Carry : Hiding Valuables and Weapons On Your Person

#51 Shoulder Holster

A shoulder holster is designed to carry large frame firearms which can be accessed easily by crossdrawing from the torso. Though this type of holster is ideal for protection when camping, hunting, hiking or fishing in the wilderness, it can also be used as a concealed carry in any scenario simply by wearing a jacket or heavy shirt overtop. A shoulder holster is often fitted with a buckle, making it easy to put on and remove, and can also accommodate other optional paraphernalia, so that you might carry more on you at once.

#52 Pocket Holster

If you're not planning to be mugged but rather would just like to keep a weapon on you in case of emergencies, you can purchase a pocket holster fitted with a hinged top flap and false brass zipper that will give the holster the appearance of a wallet in your back pocket. Using a pocket holster, you can keep your firearm on you at all times without rousing suspicion.

#53 Belly Band

With a belly band, you can conceal multiple weapons or valuables. Secured around your midsection, low on your waist and just above the belt line, a belly band can pocket handguns, cuffs, ammo, or any other weapon or accessory of choice. With adjustable holsters, you can adjust your firearm to your preferred drawing angle. The belly band is available in all sizes and is often fitted with utility pockets, meaning you can carry a variety of paraphernalia at once.

#54 Ankle Holster

Those who need a concealed carry at all hours of the day can use an ankle holster to hide their pistol or revolver in their pant leg. The band is often closed with velcro and well padded for comfort. With the additional calf strap, your ankle holster will be well secured and conveniently concealed for lightning quick speed of draw.

#55 Brass Knuckle Belt Buckle

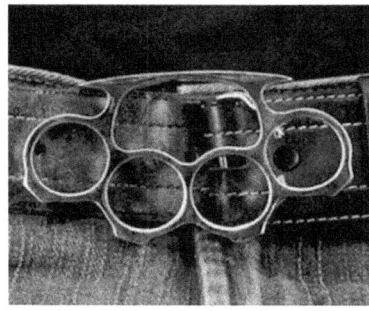

[photo credit: weapons-universe]

Believe it or not, your belt buckle can be used as a weapon...particularly if it's hiding brass knuckles in plain sight. This unique belt buckle can help you bludgeon any assailant with an iron punch. And being that the brass knuckles are concealed craftily on your belt, your assailant won't know what hit them.

#56 Day Planner Carrying Case

Your daily scheduler can house your handgun in a specially designed carrying case. The business side of the carrying case is separated from the holster compartment, allowing complete discretion. The planner is fully functional, so the carrying case won't draw suspicion, while the holster in the carrying case ensures that your firearm is secure.

#57 Inner Waistband

A hidden inner waistband holster can be worn under a tucked-in shirt, concealed from passersby. Often built of leather, the belt attachment uses metal clips or loops, and sometimes fits between the pants and the belt with hooks that attach the holster to the belt. A pistol can be concealed under a shirt, jacket, or suit, and drawn by lifting the shirt and gripping the pistol with your firing hand.

#58 Bra

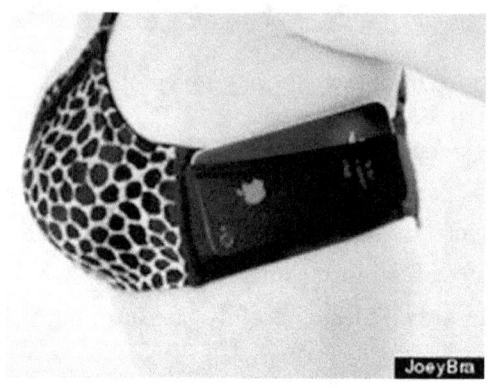

[photo credit: huffingtonpost]

A woman doesn't have to be from the 1920's to slip cash in her bra for safe keeping. Nowadays, you can buy a bra that's built specifically to store your valuables, whether they be a few bills or an iPhone. The JoeyBra, pictured above, was a kickstarter project launched by a couple of university students. Whereas many of the modern day security bras offer pockets on the chest, this one secures your valuables on the side, under your arm, providing extra security.

#59 In Hair

You, too, can be some sort of femme fatale from an action drama by hiding your weapon in your hair. Fit an ornamental hairpin with a sharp end, like a dagger, into your bun or hairdo. You can either buy a hairpin specifically designed to be used as a weapon or simply utilize whatever sharp and incisive object you have on hand to pin up your hair in the event that you need to stab someone in the eye with a knitting needle.

#60 Mace Keychain

A pepper spray keychain is a must for any woman who has a late night job. Pepper spray is composed of an element gleaned from cayenne peppers, called oleoresin capsicum. If you've ever eaten one of these peppers, you can imagine the burning sensation that a spray composed of this element would induce. Appearing as though it's a simple keychain attachment, this concealed weapon can be carried on you at all times, with the potential to thwart any attacker when sprayed at their eyes, skin or throat.

Chapter 4:
Online Vault: Hiding Your Digital Foot Print

Publishing

#61   Wikileaks

WikiLeaks allows users to securely submit censored or classified material that's ethically, politically or diplomatically significant. In submitting material, users are protected by law and by the site's bank-grade encryption. As the site is under Swedish and Belgium press secrecy laws, no logs are kept. Users can submit their information using the TOR network, which offers maximum security and complete anonymity. Wikileaks also provides a secure chat room, which protects user identity and is secured through SSL encryption. With accredited journalists on staff, a journalist-source relationship is honored with each online submission. Wikileaks has produced more than 100,000 articles world-wide, protecting every source, providing completely uncensored materials, and defeating any legal attacks against the publication.

VoIP/Video Messaging

#62   Jitsi

Compatible with Windows, Linux and OSX, Jitsi is open source software that provides audio and video encryption, as well as encrypted password storage, encrypted instant messaging, chat authentication, and call encryption.

Meshnet (decentralized networks)

#63   Commotion

Wireless mesh networks enable wireless devices to connect to one another without traveling through a centralized network. Using computers, mobile phones and wireless devices, this free, open-source communication tool produces decentralized mesh networks by enabling your trusted contacts to share your Internet connection and other applications. Commotion aims to create a platform that prevents surveillance so that wireless network communities can be built and local applications can be hosted.

#64   GNUnet

GNUnet offers peer-to-peer networking without using centralized networks or services. The free software aims to enable a global network framework that secures privacy through anonymous uncensored file-sharing. GNUnet's other applications provide building blocks for secure networking applications; for example, the GNU Name System application is a decentralized public key framework that helps to preserve privacy.

#65   Hyperboria

This global decentralized network of "nodes" running cjdns software, offers an Internet alternative. The alternative provides strong security through its decentralization. If a user wants to participate in the network, all they have to do is locate a peer who's connected.

Search Engines

#66 ixquick

This search engine doesn't track your searches, use tracking cookies, or store your IP address. No information about the user is required by ixquick. Free protection is provided using strong SSL encryption, which prevents surveillance by everyone – from hackers to the federal government. Ixquick does this by submitting your search query anonymously to various search engines and providing the results to you privately. Not only is your search private, but the pages can be viewed securely and, unlike with other search engines, the results are not filtered.

#67 DuckDuckGo Search and Stories

Compatible with Android, this search engine doesn't track users, allowing complete privacy and security, and no filtering or censorship. Offering users hundreds of answers to their searches, the engine's !bang command directs your search to thousands of additional sites.

Virtual Private Networks (VPNs), Internet Anonymizers, and Proxy Servers

#68 Tails

The goal of this free software is to preserve user anonymity and privacy. Tails circumvents censorship and provides online anonymity so that users can go anywhere without being tracked. The complete operating system is independently accessed via a USB stick, DVD or SD card, as opposed to accessed through the computer's operating system. Built-in applications, like instant messaging, email, a web browser, an image and sound editor, and office suite, are pre-configured to provide the ultimate security. With state-of-the-art cryptographic tools, Tails connects to the Internet using Tor, an anonymous network that provides online privacy.

#69 Tor

Compatible with Windows, GNU/Linux, OSX, BSD, and Unix, Tor was initially designed to protect government communications – in particular, the U.S. Navy's. Presently, everyone from the military to journalists to everyday Joe Schmos uses Tor to protect their online privacy and security. With a wide range of applications, Tor enables users to share information on public networks securely and overrides censorship so that users have access to sites that are blocked by local Internet providers. Users are also protected against "traffic analysis," so that third parties aren't provided personal information and data.

#70 Orbot

This free proxy app is compatible with Android and encrypts a user's Internet traffic by way of Tor. Orbot's open network secures its users' confidential activities and offers privacy from tracking. By bouncing its users' encrypted traffic around the world via networks of computers, identity protection is virtually ensured.

#71 Anonymizer

Compatible with OSX, Windows, Linux, iPad, iPhone, and Android, Anonymizer secures its users' online activities by encrypting their Internet traffic. In this way, users can feel secure when they access WiFi hotspots, as their identity will be protected, and their searches will be anonymous. A user's true location and IP address is masked, allowing them to view uncensored content.

#72 CyberGhost

CyberGhost protects your identity when surfing the web by providing an anonymous IP address that offers security and privacy. You won't be tracked by the government or rogue entities, and your passwords and other valuable online details won't be at risk. This VPN is great for when you're using the Internet in a public venue, like at an Internet café. CyberGhost also enables you to surf the uncensored web, allowing you to access content that may otherwise be blocked. Being invisible on the web has additional perks, such as keeping threats at bay. CyberGhost does this by providing a Firewall to each server, filtering ingoing data traffic. On top of that, the VPN's data compression allows its users to access websites up to 30% faster than without it.

Antivirus Software

#73 AVG

AVG Internet Security can be used for home or business to prevent or eliminate spam, viruses, Trojans and spyware. When users instant message or surf the web, phishing, rootkits, identity theft, and other harmful web exploits are rendered ineffective. AVG secures everything users do online, including banking, shopping, downloading and sharing files. Local Area Networks are also protected against harmful system attacks. New features, such as the AVG Accelerator and the AVG Advisor, speed up downloads and Flash videos, and provide advice when memory problems due to browser sessions are detected. All in all, the software makes Internet use safer and faster.

Web Browser Ad-ons

#74 Adblock Plus

Blocking irritating ads on compatible web browsers (Firefox, Opera, Chrome, Android), Adblock Plus is the leading browser extension in the world. The open source project has been around since 2006. Through filter lists, the software blocks certain elements of websites, like advertisements, malware, and tracking.

#75 HTTPS Everywhere

Compatible with Chrome, Firefox and Opera, HTTPS Everywhere protects the security of user browsing by encrypting user exchanges with many major websites. A number of websites default to unencrypted HTTP or link to unencrypted sites. This means the web is spotty at best when it comes to supporting HTTPS encryption. However, with the HTTPS Everywhere extension, these issues are eradicated through a smart technology which rewrites these site requests to HTTPS.

#76 Disconect

Disconect enables users of Chrome, Firefox, Safari, and Opera to be in control of their personal information by putting a halt to third party tracking sites on the Internet. The software decreases user exposure to threats, such as identity theft, malware, and the tracking of user search and browsing histories. By preventing tracking requests, Disconect also decreases bandwidth consumption, which will speed up your Internet.

#77 BetterPrivacy

Compatible with Firefox, Better Privacy protects against 'Super-Cookie's,' or special long-term cookies. Local Shared Objects (LSO) are known as flash-cookies, which are bits of information that Flash plug-ins put into your computer in central system folders. Often used like standard browser cookies, their threat potential is much more significant than conventional cookies, as they offer unlimited access to industry and market research companies to track users. The Better Privacy add-on identifies these hidden LSOs and allows users to view, manage or delete them. You can set the add-on to delete these flash-cookies automatically or manually.

Email/Communication Encryption

#78 GnuPG

GnuPG enables you to sign and encrypt your communication and data. Compatible with Windows, OSX, and Linux, the program provides free implementation of the standard OpenPGP standard, and offers features, including modules that allow you to access all varieties of public key directories. The program integrates easily with other applications.

#79 Mailvelope

Compatible with Firefox and Chrome, Mailvelope utilizes the standard OpenPGP encryption, so that all existing email encryption solutions can adapt to it. The program integrates into the email user interface, so it does not limit the normal workability of your email. If you install the program from the Chrome Web Store, then the installation package will be signed, verifying its origin and authenticity.

#80 GPGMail

As a plug-in for Apple Mail, GPGMail encrypts and

verifies mail and files that are shared between you and your contacts. The open source implementation requires GPG keys, and the GPG Keychain Access allows you to manage these keys and import those of your friends'. You simply input your name and the email address you'd like to use, and you'll be given a key which you can upload to a key server, where it will be available to your friends.

Alternative Email Accounts

#81 Guerrilla Mail

Offering disposable email addresses, Guerrilla Mail requires no registration, simply divying out a random address to users or providing an address of the user's choice. If you don't trust an individual, organization or website which requires an email, you can offer them your Guerrilla Mail address, open their sent email and confirm, then delete the account. You'll never see spam in your mailbox, as any sent to the disposable account will be deleted.

#82 NeoMail

For over ten years, NeoMail has been enabling organizations and individuals to secure their virtual privacy by offering services for both secure email and private surfing. The email service provides multi-level security, spam and virus protection, disposable addresses, and IP anonymity, while the private surfing service allows users to search with IP anonymity and SSL security, protecting themselves from wireless attacks, identity theft, and surveillance. Hosted in Switzerland, the jurisdiction believes in high privacy and independence.

Disk/File Encryption

#83 Cryptonite

Operating with Android, Cryptonite implements TrueCrupt and EncFS so that users can open, browse, and export EncFS-encrypted files and directories in Dropbox and on their phone. Users who have phones which support FUSE (e.g. CyanogenMod) can mount EncFS and TrueCrypt volumes as well.

#84 Diskcryptor

Diskcryptor is open-source encryption software that's compatible with Windows. This free software encrypts both the system partition and all disk partitions. The old TrueCrypt format was initially designed to create empty volumes, while DiskCryptor 0.5 has been designed to encrypt partitions that already have data on them by using its own partition format. This change has boosted the stability of the program by reducing problems related to file systems.

#85 Symantec Drive Encryption

Compatible with Windows, Symantec Drive Encryption offers quality comprehensive full disk encryption for individuals and organizations. With this software, data – such as system files, user files, swap files, and even hidden files on laptops, desktops, and removable media – are all encrypted so that it's protected from unauthorized access. Customer and partner data, as well as any intellectual property will be secure. Distribution, policy creation, deployment and reporting can all be simplified through Symantec Encryption Management Server's central management.

#86 Linux Unified Key System

The Linux Unified Key System (LUKS) is free software that allows a convenient way to set up disk encryption on dm-crypt kernel module. The standard on-disk format means that it is compatible across many devices, while still providing secure multi-user password management. Data can be transferred seamlessly by all users.

#87 FileVault 2

FileVault 2 accommodates Mac products. The NSA uses this built-in encryption software for system lock down. The software secures your data by using full disk, XTS-AES 128 encryption with the possibility to encrypt your entire drive's contents. The software requires the installation of OS X Lion or later versions, as well as OS X Recovery. FileVault 2 can be enabled through the System Preference's Security & Privacy pane.

Secure Instant Messaging

#88 Cryptocat

This app works with Safari, Firefox, Chrome, and Mac, enabling easy and accessible private encrypted chat. Cryptocat's instant messaging platform works on your mobile phone or browser, encrypting every message that leaves your computer. The open source has been designed by encryption professionals and is absolutely free and accessible to everyone. You can groupchat with Cryptocat's state-of-the-art interface or send photos and files to friends with the assurance that not even the network can read your data.

#89 Off-the-Record

Off-the-Record is an encrypted communications system that works with Windows and Pidgin. By encrypting your instant messages and requiring authentication, OTR enables you to have private exchanges over instant messaging. With it's deniability feature, correspondents can rest assured that the exchanged messages are unmodified and completely authentic.

Disk/File Erasing Programs

#90 Darik's Boot and Nuke

DBAN is free erasure software which offers a self-contained bootable code that deletes the contents of attached drives. Before you recycle a computer, you can use DBAN to prevent identity theft or, if you need to remove spyware or viruses from Microsoft Windows installations, DBAN is the way to go.

#91   CCleaner

This internet history and file shredder protects your online privacy and provides a clean sweep of temporary files, history, cookies, form history, and download history on Internet Explorer, Firefox, Google Chrome, Opera and Safari. It is also a fantastic tool for cleaning Windows PC, making your computer both faster and more secure. The download is fast, and the shredder easy to use.

Password Vaults

#92 Lastpass

Lastpass is a password vault that works with Windows, Chrome, OSX, Linux, Firefox, Opera, Safari, iOS, Blackberry, Android, and Windows Mobile. With Lastpass, you can secure all sorts of information, including usernames and passwords for various websites, credit card, membership and insurance information, passport and driver's license info – whatever data needs securing, Lastpass stores it privately. You can also backup sensitive documents or images by attaching them to your secure notes. Passwords are hidden, and logins can be shared with family and friends through shared Lastpass accounts.

#93 Password Safe

Password Safe is free open source software which can be quickly installed on Windows XP, Vista, 7 and 8. Bruce Schneier, a renowned security technologist, designed this safe which allows you to easily secure hundreds of usernames and passwords in an encrypted list. Your "Master Password" will allow you to enter into your database of security passwords. This will enable you to designate various passwords to different online data systems and websites, making it more difficult for someone to see a pattern in your passwords and break into your e-mail, work, financial records, retail or other systems.

Mobile Privacy

#94 SilentCircle

Aligned with Android and iOS devices, SilentCircle encrypts text, file, video and voice exchanges. You can call anyone, anywhere – even non-members. Your end of the call will be entirely encrypted. The Out-Circle Calling feature allows you to save on your cell bill, while taking advantage of international calls and services. With the ability to select your own secure number, subscribers or non-subscribers can call you wherever you are.

#95 Chat Secure

ChatSecure is a free and open source encrypted chat client for iPhone and Android that supports OTR encryption over XMPP. ChatSecure was originally available only for iOS devices, but is now also available on Android via The Guardian Project's similar app, formerly called Gibberbot.

#96 iPGMail

iPGMail is an app for your iPad or iPhone. It allows users to send and decrypt PGP encoded messages, which ensures that messages and files will be seen or read by only their intended recipients. PGB is used worldwide to encrypt private communication, and iPGMail makes the public key cryptography available to IOS based mobile phones. Despite it's ability to encrypt, the iPGMail system does not induce limited functionality, but integrates perfectly with the iOS Mail application, and even supports DropBox so that large files can be imported and exported from the app.

#97   Wickr

Working with both iOS and Android, Wickr is a peer-to-peer encryption system that is decentralized, offering private KDC for decryption. The app encrypts your ID and device information, your data, and your password, and wipes your messages and media after they've expired. The Wickr Exchange Server interacts only with info and IDs that are hashed, such as encrypted or self-destructing text, audio and video messages and pictures. Messages are deleted from the server upon delivery.

#98   RedPhone/TextSecure

RedPhone works with Android to encrypt text and voice exchanges, as well as communication storage. The open source application is licensed and free to anyone who wishes to download it. open source application for encrypted voice and text communications.

Temporary Mobile Phones

#99   Burner Phone

Burner phones are not only applicable to mobsters, druglords or other criminal entities; they can be used in the case of one who simply would like some semblance of privacy in this modern world, where Big Brother looks too often over your shoulder. These pay-as-you-go phones provide a layer of privacy, as you can use them for whatever purpose you so choose, and then discard them.

Social Networking

#100 Buddycloud

Buddycloud offers realtime updates in a publish-subscribe format. The network is decentralized and offers strong privacy controls. Similar to Twitter, users can post status updates, moods, comments on other posts, upvotes, likes, or contribute media files. The channel posts use the open ATOM content format, though users can add other post types that support various applications.

#101 Diaspora

This alternative social media website enables users to control their own personal data. Diaspora's mission is to decentralize the social web. They believe that users shouldn't have to give up their personal information be part of an active online social community. As an open source, the software and code are absolutely free and can be hosted anywhere in the world. Users own their data, unlike with social networks like Facebook, where the company can oftentimes overstep the boundaries of privacy control.

CONCLUSION

Everyone has something to hide, whether it's sensitive information, valuable items, concealed weapons, or their virtual tracks. Though storing such things in a high security vault may be the average person's first choice, safes command a thief's attention, as they most certainly house items of value. So why spend a fortune on a safe when there are plenty of cheaper, more practical methods of hiding things, and plenty of secret hiding places already at hand? You can even fool thieves by hiding items in plain sight, as this eBook demonstrates.

This is not, by all means, a completely comprehensive list: you, too, can invent your own secret hiding places in which to store your valuables. Being that home invaders typically follow a tri-fold pattern when searching your home, you can keep their routine in mind when searching, yourself, for places to hide things. Burglars often first look for openly-displayed valuables – like the bills on your dresser or the plasma tv on your wall. Next, they search inside containers which appear as though they may house valuables – ie. a file cabinet, a lockbox, your nightstand, your jewelry box, etc. Lastly, if time permits, they conduct a deeper search in likely hiding places – under your mattress, in your sock drawer, at the back of your closet, etc.

Though you obviously want your invaders to leave

empty-handed, as suggested in the introduction, you might fake your intruders out by offering a few false stashes so that they're satisfied and aren't inclined to search further. Divert your thief's attention by setting a mug full of coins out on display or cheap jewelry that looks like something of value. Though you may not be able to fool professionals, amateurs will think they've struck gold.

With enough time and enough brains, anything can be found...but thieves usually have neither. Creating the perfect hiding place may be impossible, but with the 101 secret hiding places offered in this book, you can most certainly thwart the common thief and maybe even the not-so-common one. Secret hiding places to utilize as you travel will provide some security on-the-go, while concealing a weapon or valuables on your person will offer further protection against those who wish to cause you harm. And, lastly, hiding your digital footprint has never been easier with the available software and apps designed to do just that. With a little effort and ingenuity, you can hide your valuables, your weapons and your identity from anyone, anywhere, anytime.

DISCLAIMER AND/OR LEGAL NOTICES: Every effort has been made to accurately represent this book and it's potential. Results vary with every individual, and your results may or may not be different from those depicted. No promises, guarantees or warranties, whether stated or implied, have been made that you will produce any specific result from this book. Your efforts are individual and unique, and may vary from those shown. Your success depends on your efforts, background and motivation.

The material in this publication is provided for educational and informational purposes only and is not intended as medical advice. The information contained in this book should not be used to diagnose or treat any illness, metabolic disorder, disease or health problem. Always consult your physician or health care provider before beginning any nutrition or exercise program. Use of the programs, advice, and information contained in this book is at the sole choice and risk of the reader.